Ninja CREAMi Cookbook for Beginners

Donatella Williams

D1521020

Introduction

The treat known as the ice cream is enjoyed by people all over the world. However, although there are many different flavors and varieties available, there hasn't always been an easy way to make your own at home.

Large and unwieldy, the first hand-crank ice cream makers were difficult to store and operate. In addition, the process was labor-intensive and time-consuming. In fact, making ice cream by hand usually necessitated at least three people with strong arms!

It was necessary to first prepare a custard mixture, which was then required to be chilled overnight. You then had to assemble the machine, add rock salt and ice outside the vessel, which was messy and difficult, pour in the custard mixture, and crank the handle until the ice cream frozen, which took a while. For the ice cream to not become too hard, you had to keep adding more rock salt and water as it melted. You also had to watch the paddle to ensure it didn't get too hard or melt too much ice cream. Finally, the ice cream had to "ripen" in the freezer for at least eight hours after it had been churned before it could be served. Although the results were delicious, it was sometimes just easier to go to the store and buy ice cream, even if the flavors weren't nearly as interesting as those made at home.

This came to an end with the introduction of electric ice cream makers. Still, the first models were so noisy that many families chose to leave them outside while they worked, much to the chagrin of their neighbors. Although they were smaller and less cumbersome than their hand-cranked counterparts, these electric ice cream makers were no less difficult to use, as they still required the addition of rock salt and ice.

However, with the introduction of new electric ice cream makers with freezer inserts in the 1980s, the world of homemade ice cream underwent a significant transformation. These modern ice cream makers are simple to operate and significantly more efficient than older models, thanks to freezing the base container and eliminating the need for rock salt. A blender or food processor, on the other hand, is required for more complicated recipes such as a milkshake or a smoothie bowl, among other things. Alternatively, a gelato maker.

That is no longer the case!

The Ninja® CREAMiTM, with its simple design and numerous functions, has completely transformed the world of homemade ice cream and other frozen treats into something new. It is extremely enjoyable to use, and it necessitates no special equipment. You can host the perfect ice cream social any day of the week as long as you have measuring spoons and cups, a freezer, and a Ninja® CREAMiTM machine on hand.

CREAMi is also the perfect size—almost it's as big as a single-serve coffee maker, which is a nice touch. In minutes and with minimal effort, you can create a variety of flavors of ice cream, gelato, and sorbet using multiple CREAMi Pints.

Do you enjoy ice cream flavors that are out of the ordinary, such as licorice or lemon, as well as mix-ins such as peanut butter cups or chocolate chips? It's no longer necessary to go out in search of your favorite flavors; instead, you can create them at home with your Ninja® CREAMiTM and this cookbook.

In addition, the Ninja® CREAMiTM allows you to personalize your homemade ice cream to suit your own preferences and mood. Do you enjoy ice cream with a variety of toppings? On the CREAMi, this is a piece of cake, thanks to the Mix-In feature. For breakfast, how about a delicious smoothie bowl with fruit and yogurt? That can be accomplished through the use of the CREAMi function as well.

The best part is that you have complete control over what goes into your frozen treats, which is especially important if you or a member of your family has food allergies or dietary restrictions. With a little tweaking, you can make your ice cream with nondairy milks (coconut milk, soy milk, or almond milk, for example), experiment with different types of sweeteners, and incorporate unusual ingredients such as avocados, pureed carrots, bacon, or chutney.

Simply prepare a base, combine the ingredients in the CREAM Pint, and place it in the freezer for at least 24 hours. The machine then takes over and completes the task. All you have to do is insert the pint into the machine, select the function, and sit back and watch the machine do its thing! After you've added your mix-ins (or not), your homemade creation is ready to be served.

Chapter 1: The Basics Of Ninja Creami

What Is Ninja Creami?

Introducing the Ninja CREAMi, a revolutionary new home ice cream machine that allows you to transform frozen bases into ice cream, sorbets, milkshakes, and other frozen desserts at the touch of a button. The Ninja CREAMi's proprietary technology enables the company to transform a uniformly frozen block into an incredibly smooth and creamy texture in minutes rather than hours instead of hours with other methods. This procedure is referred to as "Creamify." Your base can be consumed immediately after undergoing this transformation process, or it can be stored in the freezer for later consumption.

Parts And Pieces Of The Ninja Creami

The Ninja CREAMi comes with a base, lid, and accessories. It is recommended that you read the User Manual before using your new machine.

- The Base: The machine's base is where the frozen bases go before being turned into ice cream or sorbet or whatever treat you choose to make. The base has a sealed door so that your concoction cannot come pouring out while it is being made. It also has a drip tray underneath the base so that your delicious ice cream does not end up all over the floor.

- The Lid: The machine's lid is where you put in your frozen bases and frozen ice cream mix-ins. It also snaps down to the top of the base to keep everything in place while mixing and churning.

- The Accessories: The accessories that come with the machine include a spatula, taste spoons, measuring cup, and recipe booklet.

Main Functions Of Ninja Creami

The Ninja CREAMi's primary function is to "Creamify" a frozen base into an ice cream-like texture in 60 seconds by breaking it up and blending it together. Then you can either enjoy your CREAMified base right away or store it in the freezer until you're ready to eat it. Up to four bases can be mixed and churned simultaneously, allowing family and friends to participate in the ice cream-making process.

Here are the various functions of the Ninja CREAMi:

- MIX function: This function breaks up the frozen base into an ice cream texture. This step takes about 60 seconds.

- CHILL function: This function allows you to store your ice cream or sorbet in the machine for up to one week.

- DONE! Function: When you press this button, the Ninja CREAMi will begin blending your mix-ins with your ice cream or sorbet so that they are evenly distributed throughout the ice cream or sorbet. This process takes about 5 minutes and is called "churning." Once it is done, you can immediately serve up your delicious ice cream or sorbet or put it in containers for later enjoyment.

The Benefits of Your Ninja CREAMi

Let's look at some specific features and benefits of the Ninja CREAMi that show how special this appliance is.

Quick Processing Time

The machine chums the frozen ice cream mixture, breaking down ice crystals for the smoothest, creamiest ice cream, sorbet, and gelato.

Easy to Make Multiple Flavors

Make one basic vanilla base, then have fun creating two or three or six different flavors.

Make-Ahead Feature

You can make as many flavors of ice cream as you want ahead of time and just keep them in the freezer. Process the base in the CREAMi when you want to eat it.

Easy to Clean

All of the parts of the Ninja® CREAMi™ are dishwasher safe on the top rack, except for the part with the Dual Drive Motor. If you don't have a dishwasher, simply wash the parts with warm water and soap.

Smaller Batch Size

The smaller batch size means you don't have to store a big container of ice cream in your freezer. Just buy extra pint containers and have a tasting party or ice cream social with as many varieties as you like!

• Modes for Ice Cream, Sorbet, and Lite Ice Cream

You can make ice cream, gelato (Italian ice cream), sorbet (frozen and processed fruit or vegetable juice), and lite ice cream with just the touch of a button. Sorbets and smoothie bowls require more processing time at higher speeds to break up ice crystals for creamy results. You don't have to do any guesswork; no matter what you want to make, the machine does it all for you.

Chapter 2: Awesome Shakes

Dulce De Leche Shake

Serving: 2

Prep Time: 10 minutes

Cooking Time: 5 minutes

Ingredients:

- 1 cup vanilla or coffee ice cream

- ½ cup milk

- 2 tablespoons sweetened condensed milk

- ¼ teaspoon salt

Method:

1. Place all Ingredients into an empty CREAMi Pint.

2. Place Pint in outer bowl, install Creamerizer Paddle onto outer bowl lid and lock the lid assembly on the outer bowl. Place the bowl assembly on the motor base and crank the lever to elevate and secure the platform in place.

3. Choose the MILKSHAKE option.

4. Remove the milkshake from the Pint after the function is finished.

Nutritional Values (Per Serving)

- Calories: 125

- Fat: 9 g

- Carbohydrates: 3 g

- Protein: 8 g

Maple And Pecan Milkshake

Serving: 2

Prep Time: 10 minutes

Cooking Time: 5 minutes

Ingredients:

- ½ cup soy milk

- Pinch of salt

- 1 and ½ cup vanilla ice cream

- 1 teaspoon ground cinnamon

- 2 tablespoons maple syrup

- ¼ cup pecans, chopped

Method:

1. Make ice cream in an empty Creami Pint.

2. With a spoon, make a 12-inch-wide hole in the bottom of the pint. Fill in the rest of the ingredients in the hole.

3. Place a pint in the outer dish, place the Creamerizer Paddle on the outer dish's lid, and secure the outer dish's lid structure. Place the bowl structure on the motor base and raise and clamp the platform in place by turning the handle to the right.

4. Select the option for a milkshake.

5. Once the milkshake has been processed, pour it from the pint and serve right away.

Nutritional Values (Per Serving)

- Calories: 511

- Fat: 7 g

- Carbohydrates: 23 g

- Protein: 9 g

Choco-Hazelnut Shake

Serving: 2

Prep Time: 10 minutes

Cooking Time: 5 minutes

Ingredients:

- ½ cup whole milk

- ¼ cup hazelnut spread

- 1 and ½ cup chocolate ice cream

Method:

1. Fill an empty creami pint with ice cream.

2. Using a spoon, make a 1-inch wide hole in the bottom of the pint. Fill in the rest of the ingredients in the hole.

3. Fill the outer bowl with a pint, place the Creamerizer Paddle on the lid, and secure the lid assembly to the outer bowl. To raise and lock the platform in place, place the bowl assembly on the motor base and twist the handle to the right.

4. Choose the option for a milkshake.

5. Remove the milkshake from the pint and serve immediately after it has finished processing.

Nutritional Values (Per Serving)

- Calories: 134

- Fat: 3 g

- Carbohydrates: 22 g

- Protein: 5 g

Lemon Cookie Milk Shake

Serving: 2

Prep Time: 10 minutes

Cooking Time: 5 minutes

Ingredients:

- ¼ cup milk

- 1 and ½ cups vanilla ice cream

- 3 lemon cream sandwich cookies

Method:

1. Add ice cream, lemon cream cookies, and milk into an empty creami pint.

2. Place the pint in the outer bowl, install the Creamerizer Paddle onto the outer container lid and lock the lid component on the outer bowl. Place the bowl component on

the motor base and crank the lever to elevate and secure the platform in place.

3. Choose the milkshake option.

4. Transfer the milkshake out of the pint after the processing is done.

Nutritional Values (Per Serving)

- Calories: 431

- Fat: 24 g

- Carbohydrates: 7 g

- Protein: 9 g

Coconut Chai Milk

Serving: 2

Prep Time: 10 minutes

Cooking Time: 5 minutes

Ingredients:

- 2 chai tea bags

- ½ cup vanilla coconut milk cream

- ½ cup coconut milk

- Ground cinnamon for garnish

- Ginger for garnish

Method:

1. Introduce the coconut milk in a small pan over medium heat, simmer gently, and then take off the heat. Soak the chai tea bags inside the coconut milk until it reaches room temperature.

2. Press the tea bags into the coconut milk once it has cooled.

3. Fill an empty Creami Pint with ice cream.

4. Make a 12-inch-wide hole in the bottom of the pint with a spoon. Fill the hole with the chai coconut milk.

5. Place a pint in the outer bowl, place the Creamerizer Paddle on the outer bowl lid, and secure the lid structure to the outer bowl. Place the bowl structure on the motor base and turn the handle to the right to raise and clamp the platform in position.

6. Choose the milkshake option.

7. Once the milkshake is done processing, take out the pint, then introduce ginger and cinnamon as garnish.

8. Serve and enjoy.

Nutritional Values (Per Serving)

- Calories: 321

- Fat: 24 g

- Carbohydrates: 5 g

- Protein: 9 g

Cherry Chocolate Shake

Serving: 2

Prep Time: 10 minutes

Cooking Time: 5 minutes

Ingredients:

- 1 and ½ cups chocolate ice cream

- ½ cup canned cherries, in syrup

- ¼ cup whole milk

Method:

1. Pour all ingredients in an empty creami pint.

2. Put pint in outer bowl, install Creamerizer Paddle onto outer bowl lid, and lock the lid component on the outer bowl. Place the bowl component on the motor base and crank the lever to elevate and secure the platform in place.

3. Choose the milkshake option.

4. Remove the milkshake from the pint once the processing is done.

Nutritional Values (Per Serving)

- Calories: 231

- Fat: 12 g

- Carbohydrates: 25 g

- Protein: 8 g

Avocado "Vegan" Medley

Serving: 2

Prep Time: 10 minutes

Cooking Time: 5 minutes

Ingredients:

- 1 cup vegan coconut ice cream

- ½ cup oat milk

- 1 teaspoon vanilla extract

- Pinch of salt

- 1 teaspoon lemon juice

- 1 small ripe avocado

- 2 tablespoons agave nectar

Method:

1. Fill an empty creami Pint with all of the ingredients.

2. Put a pint in the outer bowl, then place the Creamerizer Paddle on the outer bowl lid and secure the lid structure to the outer bowl. Put the bowl structure on the motor base and turn the handle to the right to raise and clamp the platform in position.

3. Choose the milkshake option.

4. Once the processing is done, transfer the milkshake out of the pint and serve.

Nutritional Values (Per Serving)

- Calories: 100

- Fat: 16 g

- Carbohydrates: 12 g

- Protein: 6 g

Chapter 3: Perfect Ice Creams

Tooti Fruity Extract Ice Cream

Serving: 2

Prep Time: 10 minutes

Cooking Time: 25 minutes

Ingredients:

- 1 cup whole milk

- ¾ cup heavy cream

- 2 tablespoons monk fruit sweetener

- 2 tablespoons agave nectar

- ½ teaspoon raspberry extract

- ½ teaspoon vanilla extract

- ¼ teaspoon lemon extract

- 5-6 drops of blue food color

Method:

1. In a bowl, add all Ingredients and eat until well combined.

2. Transfer the mixture into an empty Ninja CREAMi pint container.

3. Cover the container with a storage lid and freeze for 24 hours.

4. After 24 hours, remove the lid from the container and arrange it into the Outer Bowl of Ninja CREAMi.

5. Install the Creamerizer Paddle onto the lid of the outer bowl.

6. Then rotate the lid clockwise to lock.

7. Press the Power button to turn on the unit.

8. Then press the Ice Cream button.

9. When the program is completed, turn the Outer Bowl and release it from the machine.

10. Transfer the ice cream into serving bowls and serve immediately.

Nutritional Values (Per Serving)

- Calories: 322

- Fat: 4 g

- Carbohydrates: 34 g

- Protein: 6 g

Hearty Strawberry Ice Cream

Serving: 2

Prep Time: 10 minutes

Cooking Time: 24 Hours and 5 Minutes

Ingredients:

- 1 tablespoon cream cheese
- ¼ cup sugar
- 1 teaspoon vanilla bean paste
- ¾ cup heavy whipping cream
- 1 cup milk
- 6 strawberries

Method:

1. In a mixing dish, combine the cream cheese, sugar, and vanilla bean paste. Using a whisk, blend all ingredients until they are thoroughly mixed and the sugar begins to dissolve.

2. Combine the heavy whipping cream and milk in a mixing bowl. Whisk until all of the ingredients are thoroughly blended.

3. Pour the mixture into an empty ninja CREAMi Pint container. Freeze for 24 hours after adding the strawberries to the Pint, ensuring not to go over the maximum fill line.

4. Take the Pint out of the freezer after 24 hours. Take off the lid.

5. Place the Ninja CREAMi Pint into the outer bowl. Next, place the outer bowl with the Pint into the ninja CREAMi machine and turn until the outer bowl locks into place. Then, push the ICE CREAM button. During the ICE CREAM function, the ice cream will mix and become very creamy.

6. Once the ICE CREAM function has ended, turn the outer bowl and release it from the ninja CREAMi machine.

7. Your ice cream is ready to eat! Enjoy!

Nutritional Values (Per Serving)

- Calories: 222

- Fat: 6 g

- Carbohydrates: 11 g

- Protein: 6 g

Mango Ice Cream

Serving: 2

Prep Time: 10 minutes

Cooking Time: 24 Hours 5 Minutes

Ingredients:

- 1 cup milk

- ¾ cup heavy whipping cream

- ¼ cup sugar

- 1 tablespoon cream cheese

- 1 mango

Method:

1. In a mixing bowl, combine the cream cheese and sugar. Mix with a whisk until all of the ingredients are thoroughly combined, and the sugar begins to dissolve.

2. Combine the heavy whipping cream and milk in a mixing bowl. Whisk until all of the ingredients are thoroughly combined.

3. Fill an empty ninja CREAMi Pint container with the mixture. After adding the mango to the Pint, freeze for 24 hours to ensure you don't go over the maximum fill line.

4. After 24 hours, remove the pint from the freezer. Remove the cover.

5. In the outer bowl, place the Ninja CREAMi Pint. In the Ninja CREAMi machine, place the outer bowl with the Pint inside and turn until the outer bowl locks into place. Activate the ICE CREAM feature by pressing the ICE CREAM button. The ice cream will mix and become very creamy during the ICE CREAM function.

6. Turn the outer bowl and remove it from the ninja CREAMi machine once the ICE CREAM function has finished.

Nutritional Values (Per Serving)

- Calories: 229

- Fat: 9 g

- Carbohydrates: 23 g

- Protein: 6 g

Sweet Lemon Ice Cream

Serving: 5

Prep Time: 10 minutes

Cooking Time: 24 Hours 20 Minutes

Ingredients:

- 1 cup heavy whipping cream

- ½ cup half and half cream

- ½ cup white sugar

- 1 tablespoon lemon zest, grated

- 2 egg yolks

- ¼ cup fresh lemon juice

Method:

1. On low heat, whisk together the heavy cream, half-and-half cream, sugar, and lemon zest in a saucepan until the sugar is dissolved (about 5 minutes).

2. In a mixing dish, whisk together the egg yolks.

3. Stir in a few tablespoons of the cream mixture at a time into the eggs. This will assist in bringing the eggs up to temperature without them becoming scrambled. Return the egg mixture to the bowl with the cream mixture. (5 to 10 minutes of stirring until the mixture is frothy.)

4. Pour the mixture into an empty ninja CREAMi Pint container, add lemon, and freeze for 24 hours.

5. After 24 hours, remove the Pint from the freezer. Remove the lid.

6. Place the Ninja CREAMi Pint into the outer bowl. Next, place the outer bowl with the Pint into the ninja CREAMi machine and turn until the outer bowl locks into place. Then, push the ICE CREAM button.

7. Once the ICE CREAM function has ended, turn the outer bowl and release it from the ninja CREAMi machine.

Nutritional Values (Per Serving)

- Calories: 431

- Fat: 6 g

- Carbohydrates: 32 g

- Protein: 8 g

Blackberry Ice Cream

Serving: 2

Prep Time: 10 minutes

Cooking Time: 24 Hours 5 Minutes

Ingredients:

- 1 teaspoon vanilla extract

- ½ cup whole milk

- 1 cup heavy cream

- ½ teaspoon lemon zest

- ¼ cup white sugar

- ½ pint fresh blackberries

Method:

1. Puree the blackberries, sugar, and lemon zest in a blender.

2. Put the puree in a mixing bowl after straining the seeds through a fine-mesh sieve.

3. Combine the cream, milk, and vanilla extract in a mixing bowl. Mix for about 30 seconds or until the mixture is whipped. Add to the puree and mix well.

4. Pour the mixture into an empty ninja CREAMi Pint container and freeze for 24 hours.

5. After 24 hours, remove the Pint from the freezer. Remove the lid.

6. Place the Ninja CREAMi Pint into the outer bowl. Next, place the outer bowl with the Pint into the ninja CREAMi machine and turn until the outer bowl locks into place. Then, push the ICE CREAM button.

7. Once the ICE CREAM function has ended, turn the outer bowl and release it from the ninja CREAMi machine.

Nutritional Values (Per Serving)

- Calories: 321

- Fat: 5 g

- Carbohydrates: 3 g

- Protein: 8 g

Coconut Ice-cream Of Togetherness

Serving: 2

Prep Time: 10 minutes

Cooking Time: 24 Hours 25 Minutes

Ingredients:

- ½ cup sweetened flaked coconut

- ¾ cup heavy cream

- 7 ounces cream of coconut

- ½ cup milk

Method:

1. In a food processor or blender, combine the milk and coconut cream and thoroughly mix.

2. Combine the heavy cream and flaked coconut in a mixing bowl, and then add to the milk-cream mixture. Combine well.

3. Pour the mixture into an empty ninja CREAMi Pint container and freeze for 24 hours.

4. After 24 hours, remove the Pint from the freezer. Remove the lid.

5. Place the Ninja CREAMi Pint into the outer bowl. Next, place the outer bowl with the Pint into the ninja CREAMi machine and turn until the outer bowl locks into place. Then, push the ICE CREAM button.

6. Once the ICE CREAM function has ended, turn the outer bowl and release it from the ninja CREAMi machine.

Nutritional Values (Per Serving)

- Calories: 134
- Fat: 3 g
- Carbohydrates: 22 g
- Protein: 5 g

Matcha Ice Cream

Serving: 2

Prep Time: 10 minutes

Cooking Time: 5 minutes

Ingredients:

- 1 tablespoon cream cheese, soft

- 1/3 cup granulated sugar

- 2 tablespoons matcha powder

- 1 teaspoon vanilla extract

- 1 cup whole milk

- 1/3 cup heavy cream

Method:

1. Microwave the cream cheese for about ten seconds on High in a large microwave-safe bowl.

2. Remove the dish from the microwave and stir until it is completely smooth.

3. With a wire whisk, beat the sugar, matcha powder, and vanilla extract until the mixture resembles frosting.

4. Slowly drizzle in the milk and heavy cream, mixing well after each addition.

5. Fill an empty Ninja CREAMi pint container with the mixture.

6. Freeze for 24 hours after covering the container with a storage lid.

7. Remove the lid from the container after 24 hours and place it in the Ninja CREAMi Outer Bowl.

8. Attach the Creamerizer Paddle to the Outer Bowl's lid.

9. Then lock the lid by rotating it clockwise.

10. To turn on the unit, press the Power button.

11. After that, press the Ice Cream button.

12. Turn the Outer Bowl and remove it from the machine when the program is finished.

13. Place the ice cream in serving bowls and serve immediately.

Nutritional Values (Per Serving)

- Calories: 273

- Fat: 7 g

- Carbohydrates: 10 g

- Protein: 5 g

Lavender Cookies And Cream Delight

Serving: 2

Prep Time: 10 minutes

Cooking Time: 24 hours

Ingredients:

- ½ cup heavy cream

- ½ tablespoon dried lavender

- ½ cup whole milk

- ¼ cup sweetened condensed milk

- 2 drops purple food coloring

- ¼ cup crushed chocolate wafer cookies

Method:

1. Whisk together the heavy cream, lavender, and salt in a medium saucepan.

2. Steep the mixture for 10 minutes over low heat, stirring every 2 minutes to prevent bubbling.

3. Using a fine-mesh strainer, drain the lavender from the heavy cream into a large mixing basin. Discard the lavender.

4. Combine the milk, sweetened condensed milk, and purple food coloring in a large mixing bowl. Whisk until the mixture is completely smooth.

5. Pour the base into an empty CREAMi Pint. Place the Pint into an ice bath. Once cooled, place the storage lid on the Pint and freeze for 24 hours.

6. Remove the Pint from the freezer and remove its lid. Place Pint in outer bowl, install Creamerizer Paddle in outer bowl lid, and lock the lid assembly onto the outer bowl. Select ICE CREAM.

7. When the process is done, create a 1 Vfe-inch wide hole that reaches the bottom of the Pint with a spoon. It's okay if your treat exceeds the max fill line. Add crushed wafer cookies to the hole and process again using the MIX-IN program.

8. When processing is complete, remove ice cream from Pint and serve immediately, topped with extra crumbled wafers if desired.

Nutritional Values (Per Serving)

- Calories: 545

- Fat: 2 g

- Carbohydrates: 4 g

- Protein: 23 g

The Golden Rocky Road

Serving: 2

Prep Time: 10 minutes

Cooking Time: 24 hours

Ingredients:

- ½ cup whole milk

- ¼ cup frozen cauliflower florets, thawed

- ¼ cup dark brown sugar

- 1 tablespoon dark cocoa powder

- ½ teaspoon chocolate extract

- ¼ cup heavy cream

- 1 tablespoon sliced almonds

- 1 tablespoon mini chocolate chip

- 1 tablespoon mini marshmallow, mix in

Method:

1. In a blender pitcher, combine the milk, cauliflower, brown sugar, cocoa powder, and chocolate essence. Blend on high for about 60 seconds, or until the mixture is totally smooth.

2. Pour the base into an empty CREAMi Pint. Add heavy cream and stir until well combined. Place the storage lid on the Pint and freeze for 24 hours.

3. Remove the Pint from the freezer and remove the lid from the Pint. Place Pint in outer bowl, install Creamerizer Paddle onto outer bowl lid and lock the lid assembly on the outer bowl. Select ICE CREAM.

4. With a spoon, create a life-inch wide hole that reaches the bottom of the Pint. Add the sliced almonds, chocolate chips, and marshmallows to the hole and process using the MIX-IN program.

5. When processing is complete, remove the ice cream from the Pint and serve immediately.

Nutritional Values (Per Serving)

- Calories: 217

- Fat: 31 g

- Carbohydrates: 18 g

- Protein: 5 g

Vanilla Flavored Ice Cream Chocolate Chips

Serving: 2

Prep Time: 10 minutes

Cooking Time: 24 Hours And 5 Minutes

Ingredients:

- 1 tablespoons cream cheese, soft

- 1/3 cup granulated sugar

- 1 teaspoon vanilla extract

- ¼ cup heavy cream

- 1 cup whole milk

- ¼ cup mini chocolate chips

Method:

1. In a large microwave-safe bowl, microwave the cream cheese for 10 seconds. Blend in the sugar and vanilla extract with a rubber spatula until the mixture resembles frosting, about 60 seconds.

2. Whisk in the heavy cream and milk gradually until the mixture is smooth and the sugar has dissolved.

3. Fill an empty CREAMi Pint with the base. Freeze for 24 hours with the storage lid on the Pint.

4. Remove the lid from the Pint and take it out of the freezer. Place the Pint in the outer bowl, attach the Creamerizer Paddle to the lid of the outer bowl, and secure the lid assembly. ICE CREAM is the option to choose.

5. Create a 1 Vfe-inch wide hole in the bottom of the Pint with a spoon. It's fine for your treat to press above the max fill line during this process. Fill the hole in the Pint with chocolate chips and process again with the MIX-IN program.

6. Remove the ice cream from the Pint once the processing is finished.

Nutritional Values (Per Serving)

- Calories: 430

- Fat: 5 g

- Carbohydrates: 22 g

- Protein: 4 g

Chapter 4: Lovely Sorbets

Awesome Peer Sorbet

Serving: 2

Prep Time: 10 minutes

Cooking Time: 15 minutes

Ingredients:

- 15 ounces pears, in light syrup

Method:

1. Fill an empty Ninja CREAMi to the MAX FILL line with pear pieces.

2. Cover the orange slices with the can's syrup.

3. Freeze for 24 hours after covering the container with the storage lid.

4. Remove the lid from the container after 2 4 hours and place it in the Ninja CREAMi outer bowl.

5. Attach the "Creamerizer Paddle" to the outer bowl's lid.

6. Then lock the lid by rotating it clockwise.

7. To turn on the unit, press the "Power" button.

8. After that, press the "SORBET" button.

9. Turn the outer bowl and remove it from the machine once the program is finished.

10. Serve the sorbet in individual serving bowls.

Nutritional Values (Per Serving)

- Calories: 251

- Fat: 5 g

- Carbohydrates: 3 g

- Protein: 9 g

Strawberry And Champagne Delish Sorbet

Serving: 2

Prep Time: 10 minutes

Cooking Time: 24 Hours 15 Minutes

Ingredients:

- 2 ounces packet strawberry-flavored gelatin

- ¾ cup boiling water

- ½ cup light corn syrup

- 3 fluid ounces champagne

- 1 egg white, lightly beaten

Method:

1. Dissolve the gelatin in boiling water in a bowl. Beat in the corn syrup, champagne, and egg whites.

2. Put the mixture into the ninja CREAMi Pint container and freeze on a level surface in a cold freezer for a full 24 hours.

3. After 24 hours, remove the Pint from the freezer. Remove the lid.

4. Place the Ninja CREAMi Pint into the outer bowl. Place the outer bowl with the Pint into the ninja CREAMi machine and turn until the outer bowl locks into place. Push the SORBET button. During the SORBET function, the sorbet will mix together and become very creamy. This should take approximately 2 minutes.

5. Once the SORBET function has ended, turn the outer bowl and release it from the ninja CREAMi machine.

6. Your sorbet is ready to eat! Enjoy!

Nutritional Values (Per Serving)

- Calories: 494

- Fat: 14 g

- Carbohydrates: 3 g

- Protein: 12 g

Coconut Lime Sorbet

Serving: 2

Prep Time: 10 minutes

Cooking Time: 15 minutes

Ingredients:

- 7 ounces can coconut cream

- ½ cup coconut water

- ¼ cup lime juice

- ½ tablespoon lime zest

- ¼ teaspoon coconut extract

Method:

1. Combine the coconut cream, coconut water, lime juice, lime zest, and coconut extract in a mixing bowl. Cover with plastic wrap and refrigerate for at least 1 hour, or until the flavors have melded.

2. Add the mixture to the Ninja CREAMi Pint container and freeze on a level surface in a cold freezer for a full 24 hours.

3. After 24 hours, remove the Pint from the freezer. Remove the lid.

4. Place the Ninja CREAMi Pint into the outer bowl. Place the outer bowl with the Pint into the ninja CREAMi machine and turn until the outer bowl locks into place. Push the SORBET button. During the SORBET function, the sorbet will mix together and become very creamy. This should take approximately 2 minutes.

5. Once the SORBET function has ended, turn the outer bowl and release it from the ninja CREAMi machine.

6. Your sorbet is ready to eat! Enjoy!

Nutritional Values (Per Serving)

- Calories: 333

- Fat: 7 g

- Carbohydrates: 19 g

- Protein: 6 g

Mojito Sorbet

Serving: 2

Prep Time: 10 minutes

Cooking Time: 24 Hours 5 Minutes

Ingredients:

- ½ cup squeezed lime juice

- 1 teaspoon lime zest, grated

- ½ cup mint leaves, packed

- ½ cup white sugar

- ½ cup water

- ¾ cup citrus-flavored water

- 1 tablespoon rum

Method:

1. Add all ingredients to a bowl and mix until the sugar is dissolved. Pour into the ninja CREAMi Pint container and freeze on a level surface in a cold freezer for a full 24 hours.

2. After 24 hours, remove the Pint from the freezer. Remove the lid.

3. Place the Ninja CREAMi Pint into the outer bowl. Place the outer bowl with the Pint into the ninja CREAMi machine and turn until the outer bowl locks into place. Push the SORBET button. During the SORBET function, the sorbet will mix together and become very creamy. This should take approximately 2 minutes.

4. Once the SORBET function has ended, turn the outer bowl and release it from the ninja CREAMi machine.

5. Your sorbet is ready to eat! Enjoy!

Nutritional Values (Per Serving)

- Calories: 234
- Fat: 14 g

- Carbohydrates: 10 g

- Protein: 4 g

Cherry And Berry Sorbet

Serving: 2

Prep Time: 10 minutes

Cooking Time: 24 Hours 10 Minutes

Ingredients:

- 2 cups frozen cherry-berry fruit blend

- ¼ medium lemon, juiced

- ½ cup white sugar, to taste

- ½ cup rose wine

Method:

1. In a mixing bowl, combine all of the ingredients and stir until the sugar is completely dissolved. Place the mixture in the ninja CREAMi Pint container and freeze for a full 24 hours on a level surface in a cold freezer.

2. Remove the Pint from the freezer after 24 hours. Take off the lid.

3. In the outer bowl, place the Ninja CREAMi Pint. In the Ninja CREAMi machine, place the outer bowl with the Pint and turn until the outer bowl locks into place. Activate the SORBET function by pressing the SORBET button. The sorbet will mix together and become very creamy during the SORBET function. This should only take about 2 minutes.

4. Turn the outer bowl and remove it from the ninja CREAMi machine once the SORBET function has finished.

5. It's time to eat your sorbet! Enjoy!

Nutritional Values (Per Serving)

- Calories: 222

- Fat: 19 g

- Carbohydrates: 23 g

- Protein: 6 g

Hearty Banana Sorbet

Serving: 2

Prep Time: 10 minutes

Cooking Time: 24 Hours 10 Minutes

Ingredients:

- 1 Frozen Banana

- 1 teaspoon cold water

- 2 teaspoons caramel sauce

Method:

1. Place the banana, water, and caramel sauce in the ninja CREAMi Pint container and freeze for a full 24 hours on a level surface in a cold freezer.

2. Remove the Pint from the freezer after 24 hours. Take off the lid.

3. In the outer bowl, place the Ninja CREAMi Pint. In the Ninja CREAMi machine, place the outer bowl with the Pint inside and turn until the outer bowl locks into place. Activate the SORBET function by pressing the SORBET button. The sorbet will mix together and become very creamy during the SORBET function. This should only take about 2 minutes.

4. Turn the outer bowl and remove it from the ninja CREAMi machine once the SORBET function has finished.

5. It's time to eat your sorbet! Enjoy!

Nutritional Values (Per Serving)

- Calories: 261

- Fat: 8 g

- Carbohydrates: 13 g

- Protein: 9 g

Mango Sorbet

Serving: 2

Prep Time: 10 minutes

Cooking Time: 24 Hours 10 Minutes

Ingredients:

- 2 cups mango, peeled and seeded, cubed

- ½ cup simple syrup

- 1 tablespoon fresh lime juice

Method:

1. Put the fruit, syrup, and fresh lime juice into the ninja CREAMi Pint container and freeze on a level surface in a cold freezer for a full 24 hours.

2. After 24 hours, remove the Pint from the freezer. Remove the lid.

3. Place the Ninja CREAMi Pint into the outer bowl. Place the outer bowl with the Pint into the ninja CREAMi machine and turn until the outer bowl locks into place. Push the SORBET button. During the SORBET function, the sorbet will mix together and become very creamy. This should take approximately 2 minutes.

4. Once the SORBET function has ended, turn the outer bowl and release it from the ninja CREAMi machine.

5. Your sorbet is ready to eat! Enjoy!

Nutritional Values (Per Serving)

- Calories: 371

- Fat: 17 g

- Carbohydrates: 10 g

- Protein: 8 g

Peach Sorbet

Serving: 2

Prep Time: 10 minutes

Cooking Time: 15 minutes

Ingredients:

- 1 cup passionfruit seltzer

- 3 tablespoons agave nectar

- 1 can peaches, in a heavy syrup, drained

Method:

1. Combine the seltzer and agave in a mixing bowl and whisk until the agave is completely dissolved.

2. Fill an empty Ninja CREAMi pint container halfway with peaches and the seltzer mixture.

3. Freeze for 24 hours after covering the container with the storage lid.

4. Remove the lid from the container after 24 hours and place it in the Ninja CREAMi outer bowl.

5. Attach the "Creamerizer Paddle" to the outer bowl's lid.

6. Then lock the lid by rotating it clockwise.

7. To turn on the unit, press the "Power" button.

8. After that, press the "SORBET" button.

9. Turn the outer bowl and remove it from the machine once the program is finished.

10. Serve the sorbet in individual serving bowls.

Nutritional Values (Per Serving)

- Calories: 431

- Fat: 7 g

- Carbohydrates: 3 g

- Protein: 9 g

Chapter 5: Homely Smoothie Delights

Vanilla Pumpkin Smoothie

Serving: 2

Prep Time: 10 minutes

Cooking Time: 10 minutes

Ingredients:

- ¼ cup ice
- ½ cup vanilla frozen yogurt
- 4 ounces pumpkin pie spice filling
- ¼ cup flavored soy milk
- ½ teaspoon ground cinnamon
- 1 pinch ground nutmeg
- ½ teaspoon vanilla extract

Method:

1. Fill an empty ninja CREAMi Pint with pumpkin pie filling, frozen yogurt, ice, soy milk, cinnamon, nutmeg, and vanilla extract.

2. In the outer bowl, place the Ninja CREAMi Pint. In the Ninja CREAMi machine, place the outer bowl with the Pint inside and turn until the outer bowl locks into place. SMOOTHIE: Press the SMOOTHIE button. The ingredients will combine and become very creamy during the SMOOTHIE function.

3. Turn the outer bowl and remove it from the ninja CREAMi machine once the SMOOTHIE function has finished.

4. Fill a glass halfway with the smoothie.

Nutritional Values (Per Serving)

- Calories: 225
- Fat: 6 g
- Carbohydrates: 10 g
- Protein: 10 g

Healthy Avocado Smoothie

Serving: 2

Prep Time: 10 minutes

Cooking Time: 5 minutes

Ingredients:

- 8 ice cubes

- ½ cup vanilla yogurt

- 1 ripe avocado, pitted

- 3 tablespoons honey

- 1 cup milk

Method:

1. Combine the avocado, milk, yogurt, honey, and ice cubes in an empty ninja CREAMi pint.

2. In the outer bowl, place the Ninja CREAMi pint. Insert the outer bowl containing the pint into the Ninja CREAMi

machine and turn until the outer bowl is locked into place. Select the smoothie option.

3. The ingredients will combine and become very creamy during the smoothie function.

4. Turn the outer bowl and remove it from the Ninja CREAMi device once the smoothie function has concluded.

5. Pour the smoothie into glasses.

Nutritional Values (Per Serving)

- Calories: 441

- Fat: 7 g

- Carbohydrates: 3 g

- Protein: 9 g

Magical Energy Elixir Smoothie

Serving: 2

Prep Time: 10 minutes

Cooking Time: 5 minutes

Ingredients:

- ½ cup frozen red grapes

- ½ cup spring greens

- ½ cup frozen bananas

- ½ frozen pear, cored and chopped

- 2 tablespoons walnuts

- Water as needed

Method:

1. Layer the salad greens, red grapes, banana, pear, walnuts, and enough water to cover the mixture in an empty ninja CREAMi Pint.

2. Place the Ninja CREAMi Pint into the outer bowl. Place the outer bowl with the Pint into the ninja CREAMi machine and turn until the outer bowl locks into place. Push the SMOOTHIE button. During the SMOOTHIE function, the ingredients will mix together and become very creamy.

3. Once the SMOOTHIE function has ended, turn the outer bowl and release it from the ninja CREAMi machine.

4. Scoop the smoothie into a glass.

Nutritional Values (Per Serving)

- Calories: 467
- Fat: 14 g
- Carbohydrates: 23 g
- Protein: 10 g

The Mean Green Monster Smoothie

Serving: 2

Prep Time: 10 minutes

Cooking Time: 5 minutes

Ingredients:

- ½ cup baby spinach

- ½ apple peeled, cored, and chopped

- ½ banana, sliced

- ¼ cup carrots, chopped

- ½ cup fresh strawberries

- ¼ cup orange juice

- ½ cup ice

Method:

1. In an empty ninja CREAMi Pint, combine the spinach, apples, bananas, carrots, orange juice, strawberries, and ice.

2. In the outer bowl, place the Ninja CREAMi Pint. In the Ninja CREAMi machine, place the outer bowl with the Pint inside and turn until the outer bowl locks into place. SMOOTHIE: Press the SMOOTHIE button. The ingredients will combine and become very creamy during the SMOOTHIE function.

3. Turn the outer bowl and remove it from the ninja CREAMi machine once the SMOOTHIE function has finished.

4. Fill a glass halfway with the smoothie.

Nutritional Values (Per Serving)

- Calories: 224

- Fat: 8 g

- Carbohydrates: 24 g

- Protein: 6 g

Strawberry Orange Crème Smoothie

Serving: 2

Prep Time: 10 minutes

Cooking Time: 5 minutes

Ingredients:

- ¼ cup orange juice

- ¼ cup ice cubes

- ½ cup fresh strawberries, hulled

- 1 container Greek Yogurt

- 10 ounces orange crème yogurt

Method:

1. Put all the ingredients into an empty ninja CREAMi Pint.

2. Place the Ninja CREAMi Pint into the outer bowl. Place the outer bowl with the Pint into the ninja CREAMi machine and turn until the outer bowl locks into place. Push the

SMOOTHIE button. During the SMOOTHIE function, the ingredients will mix together and become very creamy.

3. Once the SMOOTHIE function has ended, turn the outer bowl and release it from the ninja CREAMi machine.

4. Scoop the smoothie into a tall glass.

Nutritional Values (Per Serving)

- Calories: 456

- Fat: 8 g

- Carbohydrates: 23 g

- Protein: 15 g

Chapter 6: Amazing Gelato

Vanilla Bean Gelato

Serving: 2

Prep Time: 10 minutes

Cooking Time: 24 Hours 5 Minutes

Ingredients:

- 1/3 cup whole milk

- 4 large egg yolks

- 1 tablespoon light corn syrup

- ¼ cup + 1 tablespoon granulated sugar

- 1 whole vanilla bean, halved lengthwise

- 1 cup heavy cream

Method:

1. In a small pan, mix the egg yolks, com syrup, and sugar until thoroughly combined and the sugar has diluted.

2. Stir together the heavy cream, milk, and vanilla bean in a hot pan.

3. Place a saucepan over medium heat and constantly stir with a rubber spatula. Cook until an instant-read thermometer registers about 165°F-175°F.

4. Take the base off the heat and strain into an empty creami Pint using a fine-mesh strainer. Position a pint of water in an ice bucket. After cooling, position the storage cap on the pint and place it in the fridge for 24 hours.

5. Transfer the pint from the fridge and the top cover from the pint. Position a pint in the outer dish, put the Creamerizer Paddle on the outer dish lid, and secure the lid setup to the outer dish. Place the bowl setup on the motor platform and turn the handle to the right to raise and clamp the platform in position.

6. Choose the gelato option.

7. Once the processing is done, you can include the mix-ins or preferred to scoop the gelato out of the pint and serve to enjoy.

<u>Nutritional Values (Per Serving)</u>

- Calories:542

- Fat: 7 g

- Carbohydrates: 5 g

- Protein: 4g

Almond Cauliflower Gelato

Serving: 2

Prep Time: 10 minutes

Cooking Time: 24 Hours 5 Minutes

Ingredients:

- ½ cup dark chocolate

- ½ cup cauliflower florets

- 2 tablespoons cocoa powder

- ½ cup heavy cream

- ¼ teaspoon almond extract

- Pinch of salt

- 1/3 cup sugar

- 1 cup whole milk

Method:

1. Combine the cocoa powder, cauliflower, almond extract, sugar, salt, milk, and heavy cream in a small saucepan.

2. In a saucepan over medium heat, cook for about 5 minutes or until the sugar is dissolved.

3. Remove the base from the heat and pour it into a creami Pint that has been left empty. Fill an ice bucket halfway with water. After it has cooled, cover the pint with the storage lid and freeze it for 24 hours.

4. Take the pint out of the freezer, as well as the lid. Place a pint in the outer dish, secure the lid component to the outer dish, and place the Creamerizer Paddle on the outer bowl lid.

5. Place the bowl component on the motor platform and raise and clamp the platform in place by turning the handle to the right.

6. Select the gelato option.

7. Using a spoon, poke a 1 1/2-inch hole in the bottom of the pint. Fill the hole with chopped dark chocolate and process with the mix-in option once more.

8. Once the gelato has been processed, scoop it out of the pint and serve.

Nutritional Values (Per Serving)

- Calories: 222

- Fat: 15 g

- Carbohydrates: 3 g

- Protein: 7 g

Blueberry Cheesecake Gelato

Serving: 2

Prep Time: 10 minutes

Cooking Time: 24 Hours 5 Minutes

Ingredients:

- 3 tablespoons granulated sugar

- ¼ cup cream cheese

- 1 teaspoon vanilla extract

- 4 large egg yolks

- 1/3 cup heavy cream

- 2 large graham crackers

- 3 tablespoons wild blueberry

- 1 cup whole milk

- 3-6 drops food coloring

Method:

1. In a small pan, whisk together the egg yolks, sugar, vanilla extract, and blueberry preserves until thoroughly combined and the sugar is dissolved.

2. Mix together heavy cream, milk, and cream cheese in a hot pan.

3. Place a saucepan over medium heat and constantly stir with a whisk or a rubber spatula. Cook until the temperature on an instant-read thermometer reaches 1650F- 1750F.

4. Take out the base from the heat and strain it into an unused creami Pint using a fine-mesh strainer. Alter the colour to your liking with food colouring. Pour a pint of water into an ice bath. After cooling, put the storage lid on the pint and place it in the freezer for 24 hours.

5. Remove the pint from the freezer and the lid from the pint. Please refer to the Quick Start Guide for information on bowl components and unit interactions.

6. Choose the ice cream option.

7. Make a 3.75cm wide hole in the bottom of the pint using a spoon. Introduce 2 graham crackers, broken into 2.5cm pieces, into the hole and repeat the mix-in process. Serve right away.

Nutritional Values (Per Serving)

- Calories: 246

- Fat: 14 g

- Carbohydrates: 12 g

- Protein: 7 g

Agave Gelato

Serving: 2

Prep Time: 10 minutes

Cooking Time: 24 Hours 5 Minutes

Ingredients:

- 2 whole eggs

- 3 tablespoons granulated sugar

- ¼ cup caramels, chopped

- ¾ cup soy milk

- ¼ cup raw agave nectar

- ½ cup unsweetened vegan creamer

Method:

1. Begin by following the package directions for making vegan eggs.

2. In a pot over medium heat, cook, occasionally stirring, until the agave begins to caramelize, about 2 to 3 minutes.

3. Remove the pan from the heat and gradually drizzle in the soy milk and vegan creamer.

4. Return the pan to low heat and whisk in the sugar and vegan eggs if used. Cook, constantly stirring, for 7 to 10 minutes, or until the base temperature reaches 175°F on an instant-read thermometer.

5. Remove from the heat and transfer to an empty creami Pint. Fill an ice bucket halfway with water. Place the storage lid on the pint and place it in the fridge for 24 hours after it has cooled.

6. Remove the pint from the freezer and remove the pint's cap. Place a pint in the outer bowl, secure the lid component to the outer bowl, and slide the Creamerizer Paddle onto the outer bowl lid.

7. Place the bowl component on the motor base and raise and clamp the platform in place by turning the handle to the right.

8. Choose the gelato option.

9. Using a spoon, poke a 1 1/2-inch hole in the pint. Fill the hole with chopped caramels and repeat the process with the mix-ins program.

10. Serve and have fun.

Nutritional Values (Per Serving)

- Calories: 221

- Fat: 5g

- Carbohydrates: 22 g

- Protein: 6 g

Pumpkin Pie Squash Gelato

Serving: 2

Prep Time: 10 minutes

Cooking Time: 24 Hours 5 Minutes

Ingredients:

- ½ cup cooked butternut squash

- ¼ cup granulated sugar

- Pinch of salt

- ¼ teaspoon allspice

- 1 and ¾ cups milk

- ½ teaspoon cinnamon

Method:

1. In a small pan, mix all ingredients and heat over medium heat for 5 minutes, or until the sugar melts.

2. Fill an empty creami Pint with a base. Position a storage lid on a pint and put it in the chiller for 24 hours.

3. Take the frozen creami out of the freezer. Put a pint in the outer bowl and install the Creamerizer. Position the paddle on the outer bowl lid and secure the lid component to the outer bowl.

4. Put the bowl component on the motor base and turn the handle to the right to raise and clamp the platform in position.

5. Choose the gelato option.

6. Once the processing is done, scoop out from the pint and serve to enjoy.

Nutritional Values (Per Serving)

- Calories: 456

- Fat: 7 g

- Carbohydrates: 12 g

- Protein: 7 g

Tripple Chocolate Gelato Delight

Serving: 2

Prep Time: 10 minutes

Cooking Time: 24 Hours 5 Minutes

Ingredients:

- 2 tablespoon chocolate chunks, chopped

- 1/3 cup dark brown sugar

- ¾ cup heavy cream

- ¾ cup whole milk

- 2 tablespoons dark cocoa powder

- 4 large whole egg yolks

- 1 tablespoon chocolate fudge topping

Method:

1. In a small pan, mix the egg yolks, sugar, cocoa powder, and chocolate fudge until thoroughly combined and the sugar is disintegrated.

2. Mix together the heavy cream and milk in a hot pan.

3. Put the pan over medium heat and stir continuously with a spatula. Cook until the temp on an instant-read 1650F - 1750F on the thermometer.

4. Remove the base from the heat and gently stir in the chocolate chunks to melt and integrate into the base; once melted, pour through a fine-mesh strainer into an empty creami Pint.

5. Put a pint of water in an ice bucket. After cooling, place the storage lid on the pint and place it in the chiller for 24 hours.

6. Remove the pint from the chiller and the lid from the pint. Put a pint in the outer dish, place the Creamerizer Paddle on the outer dish lid, and secure the lid component to the outer bowl.

7. Position the bowl component on the motor platform and turn the handle to the right to raise and clamp the platform in position.

8. Choose the gelato option.

9. When the processing is concluded, introduce the mix-ins or better RE-SPIN if preferred. Then, scoop out the gelato from the pint and serve right away.

Nutritional Values (Per Serving)

- Calories: 433

- Fat: 5 g

- Carbohydrates: 12 g

- Protein: 2 g

Red Velvet Gelato

Serving: 2

Prep Time: 10 minutes

Cooking Time: 24 Hours 5 Minutes

Ingredients:

- 4 large egg yolks

- 1 cup whole milk

- 1 teaspoon vanilla extract

- ¼ cup cream cheese

- ¼ cup granulated sugar

- 2 tablespoons cocoa powder, unsweetened

- 1/3 cup heavy cream

Method:

1. Fill a large mixing bowl halfway with ice water and set it aside.

2. In a small saucepan, whisk together the egg yolks, sugar, and cocoa powder until well combined, and the sugar has dissolved. This should not be done in a hot environment.

3. Combine the milk, heavy cream, cream cheese, vanilla extract, and food coloring in a large mixing bowl.

4. Over medium-high heat, heat the pan. Cook until an instant-read thermometer reads 165°F to 175°F, constantly whisking with a rubber spatula.

5. Remove the pan from the heat and strain the base through a fine-mesh strainer into a clean creami Pint. Place the container in the ready ice water bath with care, careful not to spill any water into the base.

6. Place the storage lid on the pint and place it in the freezer for 24 hours after the base has cooled.

7. Remove the pint from the freezer and the lid. Place the pint in the Ninja creami's outer dish, insert the Creamerizer Paddle into the outer dish lid, and secure the outer dish lid component.

8. Place the bowl component on the motor platform and raise and secure the platform by turning the handle to the right. Choose Gelato as your dessert.

9. Once the machine has finished processing, remove the gelato from the pint. Serve immediately.

Nutritional Values (Per Serving)

- Calories: 211

- Fat: 5 g

- Carbohydrates:5 g

- Protein: 6 g

Chapter 7: Amazing Gelato

Blueberry Chia Seed Lite Ice Cream

Serving: 2

Prep Time: 10 minutes

Cooking Time: 24 Hours 5 Minutes

Ingredients:

- 2 tablespoons honey

- ¼ cup milk

- 1 cup blueberries

- ½ cup vanilla Greek yogurt

- 2 tablespoons Chia Seeds

Method:

1. In a large mixing container, mix all of the ingredients and stir until smooth.

2. Fill an empty creami Pint with a base. Place a storage lid on a pint and place it in the freezer for 24 hours.

3. Remove the pint from the freezer and the lid from the pint. Put a pint in the outer dish, position the Creamerizer Paddle on the lid of the outer bowl, and secure the lid assembly to the outer dish. Place the dish assembly on the motor platform and twist the handle to the right to raise and lock the platform in position.

4. Choose the lite ice cream option. If, for some reason, some chia seeds sticks remain on the pint's sides after processing, stir, and re-spin.

5. Once the processing is done, scoop the ice cream from the pint and serve with your favourite toppings.

Nutritional Values (Per Serving)

- Calories: 222

- Fat: 5 g

- Carbohydrates: 21 g

- Protein: 5 g

Lite Apple Pie Ice Cream

Serving: 2

Prep Time: 10 minutes

Cooking Time: 24 Hours 5 Minutes

Ingredients:

- ½ teaspoon cinnamon

- 2 cups apples, chopped

- 1 teaspoon vanilla extract

- 3 tablespoons brown sugar

- ½ cup heavy cream

- ½ c up apple cider

Method:

1. Before putting a medium saucepan on the stove over medium heat, spray it with nonstick cooking spray. With 3 tablespoons of water, cook for about 10 minutes, or until the apples are soft and the water has evaporated.

2. In a saucepan, combine brown sugar, vanilla, and cinnamon. Cook for an additional 2-3 minutes, or until the apples are completely soft.

3. Transfer the cooked apple mixture to a large mixing bowl, then thoroughly combine the heavy cream and apple cider.

4. Fill a Creami Pint glass halfway with the base. Next, fill an ice bucket halfway with water. After it has cooled, cover the pint with the storage lid and freeze it for 24 hours.

5. Remove the pint from the freezer as well as the lid. Place a pint in the outer bowl, secure the lid component to the outer bowl, and place the Creamerizer Paddle on the lid of the outer bowl. To raise and lock the platform in place, place the bowl component on the motor base and twist the handle to the right.

6. For processing, select the Lite Ice Cream option.

7. Once the processing is complete, scoop it out of the pint and serve immediately.

Nutritional Values (Per Serving)

- Calories: 144

- Fat: 6 g

- Carbohydrates: 15 g

- Protein: 12 g

Lite Vanilla Coconut Ice Cream

Serving: 2

Prep Time: 10 minutes

Cooking Time: 24 Hours 5 Minutes

Ingredients:

- 14 ounces coconut milk, unsweetened

- 1 teaspoon vanilla extract

- ¼ cup stevia cane sugar

Method:

1. In a medium mixing bowl, stir in and mix the coconut milk until smooth. Then whisk in the remaining ingredients until everything is well combined and the stevia sugar has dissolved.

2. Make a base in an empty creami Pint. Place a pint in the freezer for 24 hours with a storage lid on it.

3. Take the pint out of the freezer, as well as the lid. Next, install the Creamerizer and a pint of milk in the outer dish.

4. Secure the lid component to the outer dish by placing the paddle on the outer dish lid.

5. Place the dish component on the motor platform and raise and clamp the platform in place by turning the handle to the right.

6. Select the light ice cream mode.

7. Once the ice cream has been processed, add the mix-ins or scoop the ice cream from the pint and serve.

Nutritional Values (Per Serving)

- Calories: 344
- Fat: 5 g
- Carbohydrates:2 g
- Protein: 6 g

Lite Coffee Chip Ice Cream

Serving: 2

Prep Time: 10 minutes

Cooking Time: 24 Hours 5 Minutes

Ingredients:

- 1 and ½ tablespoons instant coffee granules

- ¾ cup coconut cream

- ¼ cup chocolate chips

- 1 teaspoon vanilla extract

- ¼ cup monk fruit sweetener

- 1 cup rice milk

- ¾ cup coconut milk

Method:

1. Mix the coconut cream until smooth in a large mixing bowl.

In a mixing bowl, merge the monk fruit sweetener, stevia,

instant coffee, rice milk, and vanilla; whisk until well merged, and the sugar is solubilized.

2. Fill a clean creami Pint with the base. Then, put the storage lid on the container and put it in the fridge for 24 hours.

3. Take out the pint from the fridge and the lid from the pint. Place a pint in the outer dish, place the Creamerizer Paddle on the lid of the outer bowl, and secure the lid assembly to the outer dish.

4. Place the dish assembly on the motor platform and turn the handle to the right to raise and clamp the platform in position.

5. Choose the lite ice cream option.

6. Make a 12-inch-wide hole all the way to the bottom of the pint with a spoon. Fill the hole with chocolate chips. Then, replace the pint lid and choose the mix-in option.

7. Take out the ice cream from the pint once the processing is done. Serve to enjoy.

Nutritional Values (Per Serving)

- Calories: 225

- Fat: 4 g

- Carbohydrates: 15 g

- Protein: 6 g

Cinamon Bun Ice Cream

Serving: 2

Prep Time: 10 minutes

Cooking Time: 24 Hours 5 Minutes

Ingredients:

- 1 cup whole milk

- 1 teaspoon vanilla extract

- 1 teaspoon ground cinnamon

- 1 tablespoon cream cheese

- 2 and ½ tablespoons raw agave nectar

- ¾ cup heavy cream

Method:

1. In a large microwave-safe bowl, microwave cream cheese for 10 seconds. Then, with a spatula, stir together the agave

nectar, vanilla extract, and ground cinnamon until the mixture resembles frosting, about 60 seconds.

2. Slowly whisk in the heavy cream and milk until the mixture is completely combined and the sugar has been dissolved.

3. Make a base in an empty creami Pint. Place a pint in the freezer for 24 hours with a storage lid on it.

4. Remove the pint from the freezer as well as the lid. Next, install the Creamerizer and a pint of milk in the outer dish.

5. Secure the lid component to the outer dish by placing the paddle on the outer bowl lid.

6. Place the dish component on the motor platform and raise and clamp the platform in place by turning the handle to the right.

7. Select the light ice cream option.

8. Remove the ice cream from the pint and serve immediately after it has finished processing.

Nutritional Values (Per Serving)

- Calories: 432

- Fat: 2 g

- Carbohydrates: 5 g

- Protein: 10 g

Lite Peanut Butter Ice Cream

Serving: 2

Prep Time: 10 minutes

Cooking Time: 24 Hours 5 Minutes

Ingredients:

- 1 and ¼ cup fat-free milk

- 1 teaspoon vanilla extract

- ¼ cup stevia cane sugar blend

- 3 tablespoons peanut butter, smooth

Method:

1. In a medium mixing bowl, combine the milk, stevia blend, vanilla extract, and peanut butter until smooth, and the stevia is completely dissolved.

2. Allow the mixture to sit for about 5 minutes or until any foam has subsided. If the stevia isn't fully dissolved, stir it again.

3. Fill a clean creami Pint with the base. Position the storage lid on the container and place it in the chiller for 24 hours.

4. Take the pint out of the chiller and remove the lid. Place the pint in the Ninja creami's outer dish, insert the Creamerizer Paddle into the outer bowl lid, and secure the lid assembly to the outer dish.

5. Put the bowl assembly on the motor base and turn the handle to the right to raise and secure the platform. Choose the Lite Ice Cream option.

6. Take the ice cream out of the pint once the machine has finished processing. Serve right away.

Nutritional Values (Per Serving)

- Calories: 451
- Fat: 2 g

- Carbohydrates: 15 g

- Protein: 4 g

Lite Choco-Cookie Ice Cream

Serving: 2

Prep Time: 10 minutes

Cooking Time: 24 Hours 5 Minutes

Ingredients:

- ¼ cup crushed sugar

- 1 tablespoon cream cheese

- ½ teaspoon stevia sweetner

- 2 tablespoons cocoa powder

- 1 teaspoon vanilla

- 3 tablespoons agave nectar

- ¾ cup heavy cream

- 1 cup whole milk

Method:

1. Place the cream cheese in a large microwave-safe bowl and heat on high for 10 seconds.

2. Mix in the cocoa powder, stevia, agave, and vanilla. Microwave for 60 seconds more, or until the mixture resembles frosting.

3. Slowly whisk in the heavy cream and milk until the sugar has dissolved, and thoroughly mix the mixture.

4. Pour the base into a clean creami pint. Place the storage lid on the container and freeze for 24 hours.

5. Take the pint out of the freezer and remove the lid. Place the pint in the Ninja creami's outer bowl, insert the Creamerizer Paddle into the outer bowl lid, and secure the lid assembly to the outer bowl. Position the bowl component on the motor base, and turn the handle to the right to raise the platform and clamp it in position.

6. Choose the lite ice cream option.

7. Once the machine has finished processing, remove the lid. With a spoon, create a 1 Vfe-inch-wide hole that reaches the bottom of the pint. During this process, it's okay if your treat goes above the max fill line. Add the crushed cookies to the hole in the pint. Replace the pint lid and select the mix-in function.

8. Once the machine has finished processing, remove the ice cream from the pint. Serve to enjoy

Nutritional Values (Per Serving)

- Calories: 251

- Fat: 17 g

- Carbohydrates: 10 g

- Protein: 8 g

Conclusion

Its speed, simplicity, and portability make the NINJA CREAMI convenient for consumers and a game-changer for restaurants due to its versatility and versatility. Due to its ability to produce hundreds of servings per hour, with each batch being made to order, it should come as no surprise that so many restaurants are turning to this time-saving device.

Finally, as we near the end of this book, I'd like to offer some additional suggestions for getting the most out of your Ninja CREAMi. These include:

- To ensure long-term stability, always use ice cream bases that have been frozen. Putting a portion of your house blend in a plastic container and placing it in the freezer overnight will ensure that it freezes correctly.

- Make certain that you have thoroughly read the user guide before beginning to use the product.

- When using your bowl, always make sure that it is completely dry before using it to avoid any water splashing onto the unit while it is in use and causing damage.

- Use a clean towel to wipe down the inside of your bowl, the lid, and the paddle before each use to prevent bacteria buildup (not included)

- After each batch, it is critical to release the catch on the lid to ensure that there isn't any suction pulling the mixture into the motor, which could result in damage over time (due to excess heat).

- Always remember to thoroughly clean the unit after each and every use with warm water and dish soap.

- When the unit is in use for an extended period, it should not be submerged in water to prevent corrosion.

- Always vigorously shake the mixture before using it to ensure that any stagnant air is removed from the bowl and that all ingredients are evenly distributed throughout the bottom of the container.

- Remember to shake your Ninja CREAMi before each use to ensure that the base is evenly distributed throughout the container.

- Before using your bowl and lid, make sure that they are on a flat, level surface before using them.

- When the computer is not in use, ensure that the power cord is not pinched or resting on the ground.

- Keep in mind to turn off your unit before you walk away from it, even if it is not currently in use at the time of your exit.

- Use caution when mixing the ingredients into the base because, over time, excessive force may cause damage to the motor, resulting in shorter working periods between servicing by a Ninja technician who has been authorized to do so (due to excess heat).

- Always check around the bowl before each use to ensure there are no obstructions, such as food or foreign objects, to ensure that nothing gets stuck and causes damage to the unit while it is in use (due to excess heat).

- When frozen objects such as ice or fruit are being mixed into the unit's bowl, the unit should not be used at the same time.

- Before storing the Ninja CREAMi, unplug it from the electrical outlet and remove the base from the bowl to ensure that it does not sustain any damage due to being left plugged in and/or attached to a frozen bowl.

- Before using any product, double-check that you have thoroughly read and comprehended all safety and operation guidelines.

- Maintain control of your Ninja CREAMi at all times, whether you're operating it, removing the base for storage, or not using it. Children should never be allowed to play with or play with the device.

Sincerely appreciate you taking the time to read this book. I hope you learned something new today as a result of your experience. If you did, please make sure to share it with your friends and family so that the word can spread as well.